T 306.4 P

Mixed Messages

Interpreting Body Image & Social Norms

Mixed
Messages

Interpreting Body Image & Social Norms

by Thea Palad

Content Consultant
Vicki F. Panaccione, PhD
Licensed Child Psychologist
Founder, Better Parenting Institute

Credits

Published by ABDO Publishing Company, 8000 West 78th Street, Edina, Minnesota 55439. Copyright © 2009 by Abdo Consulting Group, Inc. International copyrights reserved in all countries. No part of this book may be reproduced in any form without written permission from the publisher. The Essential Library™ is a trademark and logo of ABDO Publishing Company.

Printed in the United States.

Special thanks to Dr. Vicki Panaccione for her expertise and guidance in shaping this series.

Coauthor: Tamra Orr
Editor: Amy Van Zee
Copy Editor: Erika Wittekind
Interior Design and Production: Becky Daum
Cover Design: Becky Daum

Library of Congress Cataloging-in-Publication Data
Palad, Thea.
  Mixed messages : interpreting body image & social norms / by Thea Palad.
     p. cm. — (Essential health: strong, beautiful girls)
  Includes index.
  ISBN 978-1-60453-102-2
  1. Body image in adolescence. 2. Self-acceptance in adolescence. 3. Teenage girls—Psychology. I. Title.

  BF724.3.B55P35 2008
  306.4'613—dc22

                              2008019351

Contents

Meet Dr. Vicki

Throughout the series Strong, Beautiful Girls, you'll hear the reassuring, knowledgeable voice of Dr. Vicki Panaccione, a licensed psychologist with more than 25 years of experience working with teens, children, and families. Dr. Vicki offers her expert advice to girls who find themselves in the difficult situations described in each chapter.

Better known as the Parenting Professor™, Dr. Vicki is founder of the Better Parenting Institute™ and author of *Discover Your Child* and *What Your Kids Would Tell You . . . If Only You'd Ask!* You might have seen her name quoted in publications such as the *New York Times*, *Family Circle*, and *Parents* magazine.

While her credentials run deep, perhaps what qualifies her most to advise girls on everything from body image to friendship to schoolwork is that she's been there, so she can relate. "I started out in junior high as the chubby new kid with glasses and freckles, who the popular kids loved to tease or even worse . . . ignore," says the doc. "They should see me now!"

Today, Dr. Vicki maintains a private practice in Melbourne, Florida, and writes articles for a variety of periodicals and Web sites. She has been interviewed or quoted in major publications including *Parenting* magazine, *Reader's Digest*, *First for Women*, and *Woman's World*, networks such as Fox, ABC, NBC, and CBS, and several popular Web sites. Dr. Vicki joined esteemed colleagues Tony Robbins, Dr. Wayne Dyer, and Bill Bartmann as coauthor of *The Power of Team*, the latest in the best-selling series Wake Up and Live the Life You Love. She is an adviser for the Web site parentalwisdom.com and also for MTV/Nickelodeon's parentsconnect.com. She is a clinical consultant for Red Line Editorial, Inc. Not to mention, she's the proud mother of Alex, her 21-year-old son who is pursuing his PhD to become a medical researcher.

With all that she has going for her now, it might be hard to imagine that Dr. Vicki was ever an awkward teen struggling to find her way. But consider this—she's living proof that no matter how bleak things might look now, they do get better. The following stories and Dr. Vicki's guidance will help you discover your own path to happiness and success, becoming the Strong, Beautiful Girl you are meant to be.

Take It from Me

Growing up, I loved pop culture. I would walk to the mall near my house and head straight for the newsstand, where I would scan the covers for my favorite celebrities. I would slowly read the magazines, rip out the posters, and wallpaper my bedroom with them. Eventually, I moved on to fashion magazines, and pictures of models replaced the teen idols. I loved it all: music videos, television shows, movies, and young adult novels. I was a pop-culture junkie.

The media I took in affected every part of my life, from the way I wore my hair to the catch phrases I used with my friends. Sometimes, the stuff I saw, heard, or read was really useful, like when it was time to shop for back-to-school clothes. Other times, the situations were so mature that I couldn't relate to them at all, and that made me feel like a little kid. At the time, I was changing so much physically and emotionally that it was hard to be comfortable and happy in my own skin. What made it worse was that I didn't see anyone who looked like me in movies, television shows, or magazines, so I felt like a total freak.

After working in magazines, I can see how the media shapes people's views. They're like the popular kids in school, telling you what's hot and what's not. What you have to realize is that there's a hidden reason behind these different media outlets. Television shows, magazines, movies, music, books, video games, advertise-ments—they're all designed to inform you, to entertain you, but most of all, to keep you spending money on whatever they are sell-ing. They shouldn't serve as a guide on how to behave, live your life, or present yourself to the world.

After you read this book, I hope you'll be able to take in all the good stuff from the me-dia while tuning out the bad. There's a ton out there to enjoy—and even more to learn—but be aware and think critically about what you take in. Understand how to do that and pretty soon, you'll be decoding the media's mixed messages.

XOXO,
Thea

1

Picture Perfect

edia images are filled with beautiful people. No one has crooked teeth, bad skin, frizzy hair, or a pooched-out tummy. It's difficult not to get down on yourself when it seems like you need to look a certain way to be rich, famous, or even happy.

Sure, these models and celebrities are more attractive than most people. But they work hard to maintain it, too. They hire private chefs, personal trainers, hair stylists, makeup artists, and wardrobe experts to keep them trim, toned, and looking great at all times. It's a stressful situation that leads many celebrities to be extremely self-conscious about their looks.

Despite all of their efforts, these media figures aren't perfect. When models are filmed or photographed, special people are hired to correct or retouch the images, so there are no wrinkles, zits, or freckles. Sometimes they even whiten teeth, shrink noses, pump up breasts, and trim waists.

The celebrities may not even look like their retouched pictures, but you'd never know it.

The celebrities may not even look like their retouched pictures, but you'd never know it. All you see is a perfect person who makes you feel bad about your own face and body. But don't buy it—it's not reality.

Just ask Vanessa. She felt so uncomfortable at a new school that she started to look to the pages of a beauty magazine for guidance. The results weren't what she had hoped.

Vanessa's Story

Vanessa had always been confident. She was smart, outgoing, athletic, and liked by practically everyone in her school. She was looking forward to starting junior high and meeting new people from other parts of town.

Unfortunately, Vanessa's first few days of school didn't go as well as she had hoped. The kids from other schools just weren't as friendly, and it was hard to make conversation with them. A month into the school year, Vanessa was psyched to hear one of her closest friends from elementary school was going to have a sleepover.

Several of the crosstown girls were invited, and Vanessa was relieved to finally have a chance to get to know them better.

Talk About It

- Did you ever have to start at a new school? Did you have a difficult time making new friends?

- Why do you think it was hard for Vanessa to make friends?

- If you were starting at a new school, what would you do to get to know other kids?

At the sleepover, Vanessa and the other girls made popcorn, watched movies, and read teen magazines. Vanessa really wasn't into magazines, so it was weird to see the other girls so interested in them. They studied the outfits, practiced the makeup tricks, and took the quizzes.

"You should wear more stuff like this—you could totally pull it off," Sara, one of the girls, said to Vanessa, as she pointed to one of the cover girls. Vanessa picked up the magazine and took a look. Was she kidding? She'd never look like this amazing creature on the cover, even if she had the same exact outfit on. But she appreciated what Sara said. And it was nice to finally hang out with some girls from her new school. Vanessa thought maybe she should start paying more attention to the magazines and their makeover tips.

Talk About It

- **Did you ever feel out of place because you didn't share the same interests with the people around you?**

- **How does it make you feel to see photos of pretty people? Do you compare yourself to them?**

- **Have you ever tried to look like a model in a magazine? Why? How did it turn out?**

Right after the sleepover, Vanessa began collecting magazines. She studied the photos at night before she went to bed, and woke up an hour early each morning to pick out her clothes and fiddle with her hair and makeup. Sometimes it took her so long to get ready for school that she'd miss the bus and end up late for homeroom.

Things got better with the crosstown girls, who were much nicer to Vanessa after the sleepover. They often complimented her on her appearance, which made Vanessa feel as if the extra hours she was putting into getting ready were worth it. But even though she was making friends, Vanessa began to feel self-conscious. No matter how early she got up to do her hair or plan her outfit, she never looked quite as good as those girls in the magazines. Vanessa thought about the way she used to dress at school. How could she have embarrassed herself like that? People must have thought she was so ugly.

Sometimes it took Vanessa so long to get ready for school that she'd miss the bus and end up late for homeroom.

Vanessa became so obsessed about the way she looked that she stopped trying to make new friends. She even felt shy around her old ones and avoided the sleepovers she enjoyed so much. She didn't want the other girls to see how hard she was trying to look perfect and how badly she was failing. Embarrassed, Vanessa kept to herself on the bus, in class, and on

the weekends. The time she used to spend hanging out with family and friends was now spent in front of a mirror, staring at the imperfections on her face and body. She missed how carefree she used to be and wished she didn't feel so self-conscious all the time.

Talk About It

- Why do you think Vanessa gave herself a makeover?

- Why wasn't Vanessa happy, even after she made new friends?

- How would you feel if you were in Vanessa's situation? What advice might you give her?

We're naturally social, so it makes sense to want to fit in with the people around us. Vanessa noticed that the group of people she wanted to be friends with valued what they saw in magazines, so she made their values her own and tried to copy the images on those pages. Unfortunately, she only set herself up for disappointment by trying to be something that didn't really exist. When Vanessa couldn't compete, she felt like a failure. This affected her self-confidence and the way she interacted with other people.

It's human nature to be competitive, but too often girls feel inferior, ugly, and fat when they start competing with celebrities and even other classmates. So whether you're comparing yourself to the coolest girl in your grade or the hottest new actress on television, just remember that no one's better at being you than you. Once you accept that you're unique and amazing, you'll be able to appreciate that other people are attractive while recognizing your own real beauty.

Get Healthy

1. If you start at a new school and have trouble making friends, don't be discouraged. Developing friendships takes time. By doing things you enjoy, such as joining a sports

team or a club, you are setting yourself up to naturally develop friendships with people who share your similar interests.

2. Instead of using pictures of models or celebrities to inspire you, tape up flattering photos of you having fun with your friends. You at your very best is a sensible goal to work toward.

3. Rather than idolizing famous people for their exterior qualities, select one that you admire for other reasons, such as her clever sense of humor, poise, or devotion to charity work. You can try to be more like her without having to change anything about your looks.

The Last Word from Thea

It's important to remember that media images are really illusions. Crews of people work hard to create pictures, so it's unfair to compare yourself to them. It's okay to want to improve yourself physically, whether it's taking extra special care of your teeth or putting more thought into an outfit. Just make sure your goals are reasonable, and that you're paying as much attention to improving your inside—your mind, body, and belief system—as you are to your outside.

2

Celeb Body

They say the camera adds ten pounds. It's difficult to know how accurate that is, but people in the public eye do live by a different set of standards when it comes to weight. What is normal and healthy in real life often "reads" as bigger in front of the camera, which is one reason why many celebrities struggle to stay so thin.

While a lucky few are naturally slim and toned, many stars put themselves on strict diets and suffer through difficult workouts to stay a certain size. The pressure to have just the right look is intense. Extreme dieting, eating disorders, plastic surgery, and alcohol and drug abuse are the unfortunate by-products of a business where dress size is sometimes more important than talent.

As a result, almost half of all girls like you are dieting or trying to change their figures to be in line with the Celeb Body. Many of you are perfectly healthy, but you end up hating your body. It's sad because the bodies that you long to have are often dangerously underfed and not so attractive when they're not in front of the camera.

Shannon felt perfectly comfortable in her own skin until she started comparing herself to the super-skinny actresses on television.

Fortunately, the focus is shifting away from starving starlets as more and more television shows, movies, and advertisements feature girls with average bodies. The success of these projects with women who don't fit the industry mold goes to show that beauty and success don't have to be restricted by weight and dress size.

Shannon felt perfectly comfortable in her own skin until she started comparing herself to the super-skinny actresses on television. She tried so hard to live up to that image that she put her own health in danger.

Shannon's Story

Shannon had always been a little bigger than the rest of the girls in her class. She was an inch or two taller, and she certainly wasn't stick-skinny, but she was never self-conscious about her body. She actually liked the way the other girls looked up to her, as if those extra inches made her older and wiser somehow.

When Shannon started developing in fifth grade, she was psyched to be the first girl in her group to get a real bra. She even got a sports bra for gym class. She was a little uncomfortable running at first, but the sports bra kept her in place so she didn't feel weird when there were boys on the track.

One morning, Shannon and her friends were gathered around her locker talking about a new episode of their favorite television show. "I love that actress who plays the girlfriend, but she looked so fat in last night's episode," one of the girls said. "I know, she's totally huge," agreed another. Shannon went red. She didn't think that actress was fat at all. In fact, the actress was thinner than she was! What did her friends think of her body, then?

Talk About It

- **Why was Shannon excited about getting a real bra?**

- **Do you think Shannon has a healthy body image?**

- **What impact do you think her friends' comments had on her body image?**

After the conversation by her locker, Shannon felt self-conscious about her height, her breasts, and most importantly, her weight. She began wearing her weekend T-shirts to school—they were much looser and hung on her body, so you couldn't really tell what was underneath. She also wore her sports bra all the time so that her breasts wouldn't look so big.

Shannon even started changing for gym class in a bathroom stall instead of the locker room. When she did have to change in front of the other girls, she would face a corner so no one could see her tummy.

At home, Shannon would hold up her shirt in front of the mirror and suck in her stomach until her ribs stuck out. She skipped dinner whenever she could get away with it, which wasn't easy to do because she'd wake up in the middle of the night with her stomach rumbling.

Talk About It

- How did Shannon's attitude about her body change? Which body parts made her feel the most self-conscious?

- Are there any parts of your body you're unhappy with? Do you ever try to disguise them?

- Have you ever skipped a meal on purpose? How did you feel afterward?

Cutting back on calories was really paying off for Shannon—she was almost always starving, but her pants did feel a little looser. It was hard to skip meals at home with her parents watching, but no one at school ever noticed if she didn't eat anything from her lunch tray. It was difficult to watch everyone around her eat, but Shannon knew how good she would feel when she looked in the mirror later.

After a month of starving herself, Shannon noticed she wasn't really losing any more weight. She didn't have much energy anymore, but she knew she had to exercise. So every day after school, she would go to the park near her house and run as much as she could. At first she couldn't do more than a mile or so, but after a few weeks she was up to three miles.

The next day, Shannon's parents took her to the doctor, who noticed right away that she was much thinner since her last physical.

Shannon was certainly smaller than she had been a few months ago. And while she was pleased with how much food she could cut out, Shannon still wasn't happy with her size. One day in class, she felt so dizzy that she couldn't focus on the papers in front of her. Shannon's teacher sent her to the school nurse, who saw that her skin was dry and her lips were chapped. When Shannon complained of weakness and chills, the nurse called her parents and told them Shannon was dehydrated.

The next day, Shannon's parents took her to the doctor, who noticed right away that she was much thinner since her last physical. After her checkup, the doctor sat down with them to discuss Shannon's dramatic weight loss. Her parents were shocked, because Shannon had been hiding her figure in big, baggy clothes. Shannon confessed that she hated her body, and that exercising and starving herself were the only things that made her feel better about the way she looked. Shannon's parents realized that their daughter had an eating disorder and serious body image issues. They turned to the doctor for a treatment plan.

Talk About It

- What was wrong with Shannon's routine?

- Were you ever unhappy with your weight?

- Did you ever see something in the media that made you feel uncomfortable about your own body? What was it?

Pressure from parents and teachers, teasing from peers, and negative media messages can make bigger girls feel bad, ugly, or ashamed. Even someone with a healthy self-image like Shannon can be derailed by misguided comments. Although she was developing faster than her friends, Shannon was comfortable with her body—until she realized that her sense of normal was someone else's idea of fat. She started trying to create the real Celeb Body, not realizing that the body image wasn't actually real at all.

While it's important to eat healthful foods and exercise regularly, doing anything to the extreme can do your body and mind more harm than good. Crash diets like the one Shannon was on don't work in the long run, and she could have done some major damage by depriving her body of important nutrition.

Rest assured that you're not alone—most of us will struggle with our body image at some point. It's not some problem that disappears on your sixteenth birthday, so it's important to develop healthy eating and exercise habits and an appreciation for your body now and maintain it for life. It's the only body you'll ever have, so why would you abuse it?

Get Healthy

1. If you want to eat better, ask your family and friends to help you change your diet. Having a support group can only increase your chances of reaching your goals, and maybe you'll inspire them to improve their diets as well!

2. Ask beautiful women you admire—your mom, your teacher, your neighbor—if they ever had to deal with body image issues. Chances are, they had their own struggles growing up. Ask them how they resolved their issues, and use their stories to help you conquer yours.

3. Don't associate unhealthy eating with having fun. Making plans to hike, skate, or ride bikes with friends takes the focus away from eating junk food and helps sneak in some physical activity as well.

The Last Word from Thea

Most of the time, the bodies we see in the media are unhealthy and misleading. Not having a Celeb Body is not a sign of failure—it means you're normal! It also shows that you're confident and smart enough to know that extreme diet and exercise is a very bad idea. Give your body a chance to figure out what's normal and healthy for you, so you can enter the adult world feeling confident.

3

American Beauty

*G*irls come in all shapes, sizes, and colors, each one uniquely beautiful. But most of us go through an awkward stage, when it seems like certain parts are growing faster than others, and features don't quite fit together like they should. During this time, it's easy to become unsure of your looks or have self-esteem issues.

The media is pretty specific about the way it defines beauty, leaving those of us who don't fall into that description to question our own appeal. Music videos feature girls with big breasts and tiny waists in belly-baring outfits. And there are shows that send a different kind of message—that glasses, braces, and conservative clothes are ugly. There are even make-over shows that convince people they're just not cute enough the way they are.

So unless you're five-foot-nine (1.8 m) and a size two, you probably won't find a lot of girls who look like you in the media. And if you have distinctive features—like a wide nose or all-over freckles—it might be difficult to be confident.

Just remember that living up to the media's standard doesn't make you a better person on the inside, which is where it really counts.

It's important to get through these years with an appreciation for your own individual beauty, regardless of what you see on-screen.

Just remember that you're pretty darn gorgeous as is, and that living up to the media's standard doesn't make you a better person on the inside, which is where it really counts. Kendra found this out for herself when she changed her trademark hairstyle just to get some attention. Read on to see why caving in to peer pressure didn't make her happy.

Kendra's Story

Kendra was an army brat. Her parents met and married overseas, and they lived in three different countries before moving to the American suburbs. She was used to going to international schools. Overseas, her classmates were all so colorful that she never even thought about being biracial herself.

But at her new school, people noticed Kendra's exotic features and often asked where she was from. She certainly didn't look like anyone else in her new school, and she loved all the attention.

Kendra met new people easily, so she had a big group of friends by the end of the semester. When summer finally came, she was excited to be going to the same sleepaway camp as many of her friends from school.

Talk About It

- **How has Kendra's viewpoint of different cultures been shaped by her experiences overseas?**

- **Did you ever stand out because of the way you looked? How did it make you feel?**

- **How do you view kids from different cultures and backgrounds?**

At camp, Kendra and her friends swam, hiked, and played volleyball. After the first few weeks, Kendra's naturally textured hair had really grown in the hot, humid weather, so she started wearing it in an Afro like her mom. She loved not having to worry about styling it, and it was easy to wrap in a bandana if it got too unruly.

One night after lights out, Kendra stayed up late laughing with her bunkmates. "Why do you wear your hair like that? Don't you get hot?" one of the other campers asked her.

"You should straighten it, or get it relaxed," a friend added. "You'd look just like the actress in that movie we saw last weekend."

Kendra had straightened her hair once before, for a cousin's wedding. It took such a long time, and she didn't look like herself, so why should she bother?

The next day, Kendra was still thinking about what her friends said. Why did they even care about her hair? Still, she didn't want them talking about her. So after lights-out, she asked if anyone had a straightening iron. "I do!" one of the girls said. "Do you want me to straighten your hair?" Why not, Kendra thought, and hopped off her bunk to sit in front of her friend.

Talk About It

- Why did Kendra like her Afro so much? Why do you think she decided to straighten it?

- Why do you think Kendra's bunkmates asked about her hair? Were they being mean, or were they just curious?

- Have your friends ever tried to get you to change something about your looks? How did it make you feel? Did you do it?

It took a really long time, but they finally straightened all of Kendra's hair. She had to prop her head up on a pillow to avoid messing it up, so she barely slept a wink that night. But the next morning, Kendra unveiled her smooth, straight do—she did look like that actress! She decided to keep her new style for good, or at least until school started again. It was hard, though, and Kendra found herself sitting out of a lot of the fun activities so she wouldn't mess up her hair or start sweating and have it frizz.

When Kendra came home from summer camp, she was excited to show her parents her brand-new look. But when they saw her, they were less than thrilled. "What'd you do that for?" her mother asked. "You have such naturally beautiful hair—it was your trademark."

"You look very nice, Kendra, but you don't look like yourself," her father added. Kendra was bummed at her parents' reaction, but what did they know?

When school started, Kendra waited for the compliments to come, but everyone reacted the way her parents had. Kendra just did not get it. She had this amazing, shampoo-commercial hair now, but all anyone could talk about was her old, frizzy hairdo. What was up with that? That night, Kendra studied her reflection in the bathroom mirror. She literally looked like she could have been in a magazine. So why wasn't she happy?

When school started, Kendra waited for the compliments to come, but everyone reacted the way her parents had.

Talk About It

- Why didn't Kendra's parents like her new hairstyle? Why do you think she blew off their comments? Do you think she really cared about what they said?

- Why is Kendra unhappy? What advice do you have for her?

- Have you ever tried to change your looks? How did people react? How did you feel?

When you watch movies or open a magazine, you often see variations of the same American Beauty. Most of you don't look anything like this girl, and that's okay. Imagine how boring the world would be if everybody looked the same. Fortunately, we come in a wide range of shapes and colors, and who's to say what's more beautiful anyway? Just like your taste in music, clothes, and food, beauty is totally a matter of opinion, and not everyone is going to have the same taste.

Keep that in mind the next time you're comparing yourself to an American Beauty you see on television or in a magazine. So what if she is gorgeous? That doesn't make her a better person than you, nor does it make you any less attractive. Most girls your age have days when they just don't feel good about their looks. It's normal to be a little stressed when you're having a bad hair day or when nothing you put on looks right. Just don't get hung up on those days! A bad hair day is just that—a day, not your entire life! No one looks his or her best all the time. Just ask the stars who have to live with the photographers trying to catch them without makeup, with visible panty lines, or with bulging tummies. So give yourself a break—nobody's perfect.

Get Healthy

1. Look through photos of your friends and pick out each girl's best physical feature. Compliment her on it the next time you see her.

2. Go through magazines and rip out pictures of women who are uniquely pretty. Look for girls with something different, such as the texture of her hair, the size of her nose, or the shape of her eyes.

3. Read celebrity interviews in magazines, in newspapers, and on Web sites. Stars often talk about the body parts they hate, or how awkward they felt while growing up. It goes to show that everyone—even the rich, famous, and beautiful—feels unsure of her looks sometimes.

The Last Word from Thea

Despite what you see in the media, beauty can't be defined by a certain image. It's easy to feel down about the way you look when you don't see faces similar to yours in magazines or advertisements. Just remember that the media isn't there to make you feel good about yourself. Don't buy into claims that promise to transform your hair, skin, or style. Good grooming and hygiene, along with a healthy mind, body, and attitude, are the only beauty tricks you need to know.

4

Not So Fast

Many girls regularly watch teen dramas on television. Week after week, hot stars act out racy plot twists involving juicy scandals and secrets. But did you ever wonder how these characters—who were supposed to be your age—have all this freedom? Where did they get all their money? How were they getting into clubs and going out on school nights without their parents' permission? And when did they do homework?

Sometimes, it's hard to separate real life from what you see in the media. The people who make these shows want you to keep tuning in, so they spice up their story lines with sex, drugs, and alcohol—which is not reality for most girls your age. In addition, the actors playing these parts are often much older than the characters they portray, so it's no wonder they look and act much older than you. These shows make it seem like it's a bad thing to act your age and make wise decisions. But what's the rush to grow up?

Don't compare your life to the stuff you see in the movies or on television. Just think about it: 5-year-olds, 10-year-olds, 15-year-olds, and 20-year-olds all have very different ideas of fun. You develop different tastes as you mature, so why not go at a pace that's right for you?

Erica's Story

Erica had always been small. Even though she was the same age as everyone in her class, she was the shortest and skinniest. Because she was so tiny, everyone—including her classmates—treated her as if she were younger. People babied her because they **Don't compare your life to the stuff you see in the movies or on television.** assumed she couldn't take care of herself, even though Erica was probably the smartest person in her grade.

Erica loved reading and watching television. She was really into game shows, but her older sister was into soap operas and teen dramas, and she never missed an episode. Erica didn't have a television in her room, so when she finished her homework she had to sit through her sister's shows.

Talk About It

- Why did people assume that Erica couldn't take care of herself?

- Do you ever assume things about people based on how they look? Do you think people assume things about you?

After several weeks of watching her sister's shows, Erica really got into them, especially the one where the kids went to a really ritzy private school. The characters were all so gorgeous and lived such exciting lives.

There was always drama, and they did cool things such as going to spas and shopping in the city.

Erica didn't always want to do the same things they did, but she did want to go to the mall with her friends and have her own MySpace account. She suddenly resented her mom for keeping her on such a tight leash. She wasn't a baby, so why was she being treated like one? Erica had always been responsible—didn't that count for anything? And it's not like she wanted to get into trouble; she just wanted to have fun, like the kids on her favorite show!

Erica thought of ways to convince her mom, classmates, and teachers that she wasn't a little kid anymore. She figured if she looked more mature, people would start treating her that way. Erica asked her older sister if she could borrow her shoes and makeup, and then she went to work on her grown-up look.

Talk About It

- How did watching television shows affect the way Erica felt about her parents?

- Do you ever resent your parents for not letting you do what you want? Do you do anything about it?

- What are some other ways Erica could convince others that she is more mature, rather than through clothes and makeup?

The next Monday, Erica arrived at school in her sister's three-inch heels. She also wore mascara and shiny lip gloss. Everyone in her class noticed, especially her teacher, who called Erica up to her desk. "Is everything okay?" she asked Erica. "Yeah, totally," she answered, trying to make her voice sound lower and more mature.

At lunch, Erica felt self-conscious as she crossed the cafeteria with her lunch tray. People were noticing her new look—which was good—but she was definitely uncomfortable. She was on her way to her usual spot when a group of

Erica desperately wanted to jump into the conversation, but she had nothing to say. She had zero in common with these girls!

older girls asked if she wanted to eat at their table. Erica's heart was doing backflips inside her chest, but she played it cool and sat down casually.

Erica spent the rest of her lunch period listening to the other girls talk about their breasts, periods, and house parties. She desperately wanted to jump into the conversation, but she had nothing to say. She had zero in common with these girls! She didn't have breasts or her period—and she had never been to a house party. Erica felt like even more of a baby than she did around her classmates. She definitely wasn't ready for this stuff. As she gathered her tray and left the table, Erica decided to dress like herself the next day.

Talk About It

- Why do you think the older girls invited Erica to sit at their lunch table? How do you think Erica felt to be asked?

- Why do you think Erica felt worse, even after getting approval from the older girls?

- Did you ever find yourself in a situation that made you feel uncomfortable, or where you didn't fit in? What did you do?

Everyone wants to be taken seriously, and no one wants to be treated like a little kid. But when your physical appearance and your maturity levels don't match, you have to fight that much harder to get people to see you and what you're capable of doing. It's not impossible, but it is challenging, so you have to be smart about your approach. Just changing your appearance isn't going to change a person's mind. You have to show them through your words and actions that there's more to you than meets the eye.

That said, you have the rest of your life to be an adult—and take on all the responsibilities that go along with being older—so what's the rush? Sure, being mature means having the freedom to do the stuff you want. But maturity also means that you're able to make smart, informed decisions about your life. At this age, you're still learning how to balance what you want to be doing with what you should be doing, which isn't an easy lesson to learn.

Get Healthy

1. Listen to your parent's viewpoints when they say something isn't a good idea. But if you feel strongly about something, discuss it with them calmly and rationally. Don't argue or get emotional—just present your case and let your maturity persuade them.

2. Trust your instincts. If you're uncomfortable with someone or something, then the situation probably isn't right for you and you should get out of it. Rather than feeling shy or embarrassed about your reaction, be proud of yourself—not everyone is strong or smart enough to recognize when something's not for them.

3. Don't let yourself be bullied, and don't let the media or your friends convince you to do something that you wouldn't do on your own. Practice saying no firmly, so those around you know you won't be pressured.

The Last Word from Thea

Life isn't a race, and it would be unfair to ask you to keep up with some fictional television characters that were created to be entertaining. You only have so many years to grow up and figure out who you are and what you believe in—don't fast-forward through this process. Besides, in the real world, not only do you get to do cooler stuff as you get older, but you also get more responsibilities. Television shows will tell you that growing up only means having more fun, but the reality is that growing up means harder schoolwork, higher expectations, and more responsibilities. So take the time to enjoy the benefits of being your age, while you look forward to the privileges—and work—of being older.

5

Breaking Molds

*L*ook around at your classmates. Do the smart people stick together? Do the athletes? How about kids from other countries? It's easy to make friends with people you have something in common with, and it's simple to label someone you don't know into a neat little category. The hard part is seeing past those initial stereotypes.

The media promotes stereotypes, including generalizations about gender, religion, and ethnic groups. Television shows do it all the time, assigning people identities such as the nerd, the hippie, and the geek. These shows teach you to judge people quickly based on their looks, without knowing anything about them.

When this habit spills into real life, you'll end up shortchanging your peers with preset notions of who they are just by how they appear on the outside. It takes courage to go beyond your comfort zone and approach people with whom you have no common interest. But if you never venture out, you're missing the chance to make some great friends and experience cool things. Having a varied group of friends keeps you from making snap judgments about other people—and prevents others from stereotyping you, too.

> **It takes courage to approach people with whom you have no common interest.**

Sadly, some adults have never learned this lesson and take stereotypes to heart. They assume they know a person based on the way she looks, and it's this kind of thinking that leads to sexism, racism, and prejudice. You can do your part by not making broad generalizations about any group, and by taking the time to get to know people outside your clique. Maybe you'll inspire others to wander outside their comfort zones, too.

Marya was tired of people treating her like someone she wasn't. She quickly learned that one dramatic step was enough to help change how others saw her.

Marya's Story

Marya did not look like most kids in her school. She wore dark purple lipstick and colored her nails with black markers. She didn't have a lot of clothes that she loved, so she wore her favorite things—mostly black—over and over again. People assumed she was Goth.

Teachers thought Marya was a troublemaker too, even though she was hardworking and took her schoolwork very seriously. Sometimes they accused her of disrupting the class when other students got too rowdy. Marya would just sigh, sink deeper into her chair, and focus on the work in front of her.

Marya had just one close girl friend, Michaela. She and Michaela didn't have very much in common—in fact, they never even talked outside of school. They drifted toward each other since they sort of had the same Goth look. They had one other guy friend, Ephraim, who was one grade ahead. Ephraim wore black eyeliner and a black trench coat, even in the summer.

Talk About It

- What stereotype did people give Marya? Why? Why did teachers assume she was a troublemaker?

- Do you think that people stereotype you? What do you think they assume about you? Are they right?

- Do you stereotype other people? Why?

People thought she was a mope, but Marya was really just quiet. Whenever anyone actually talked to her, she was quite friendly. Still, people never came up to her if they didn't have to. This bugged Marya, so she thought about joining some clubs to make new friends.

Marya had taken dance and gymnastics classes since she was three years old, so she was sure she'd be a good cheerleader. At tryouts, the other girls were shocked to see Marya there in her usual black outfit. There was a lot of whispering and snickering, but Marya was used to it at this point. They did some drills and practiced simple cheers, routines, and stunts. To

People thought she was a mope, but Marya was really just quiet.

everyone's surprise, Marya caught on quickly and performed with energy. "Wow, she's awesome. Who knew?" one of the older cheerleaders commented.

A week later, Marya was thrilled to find out she had made the team. But even though she made a little progress during tryouts, the other girls still weren't friendly to her. And when she told Michaela and Ephraim about making the team, they just rolled their eyes.

The weekend before practices started, the team had a sleepover so that everyone could get to know each other better. Without her makeup, Marya looked just like the other girls in her pajama bottoms and tank top. Still, no one really talked to her. "So . . . why are you doing this exactly?" one of the girls finally asked Marya. "Are you, like, planning to sabotage the team or something?"

Talk About It

- Why was everyone surprised by Marya's tryout?
- Do you think Marya has a healthy attitude about her stereotype? Why or why not?
- Have you ever tried to join a group that wasn't very accepting of you? How did you deal with it?

Marya was shocked. She had no idea these girls, like her teachers, assumed she was a bad kid. She just had to laugh because it was so ridiculous. "Whatever! I've always wanted to cheer. I was just afraid to try out," Marya explained. "I'm not evil or anything—I just really like to wear black! I'm into the same things you guys are." The other girls were quiet at first, but by the end of the sleepover, the girls were treating Marya like anyone else on the team.

Though her new teammates had accepted her, Marya had a hard time getting Michaela and Ephraim to support her new role as a cheerleader. "I can't believe you're actually doing this. Will you morph into a Stuck-up like the rest of them?" Ephraim asked.

"You're way off," Marya defended. "Most of them are really nice. One of them even said you were cute!" Ephraim blushed furiously and stopped his attack on the cheerleaders. At her very first game, Marya was thrilled to see both of her friends in the bleachers, cheering her on.

Talk About It

- Do you think Marya handled the sleepover situation well? Why or why not?

- Why do you think Michaela and Ephraim were so against Marya joining the cheerleading team? Did they have their own stereotype for cheerleaders? For Marya?

Growing up, everyone just wants to fit in. No one wants to be the outcast, so people look for others who look, dress, or act the way they do—there's safety in numbers. While it's great to hang out with people who have something in common with you, sometimes being part of a group can be a bad thing if you stop having your own ideas. And when others only see you as a member of a group instead of as an individual, it can be a disadvantage to you.

There are times when you do want to be recognized for your ideas and talents apart from the crowd. Some people judge you based on the people you hang out with, so it's important to maintain your individuality. It's also important for you not to judge others based on the groups they belong to. Just like you, they have many different hobbies and interests, and it would be unfair of you to make up your mind about them without getting to know them first. So take the time to wander outside your social circle—you might end up with some amazing friends who open your eyes to new things you'd never know about if you only stayed inside your comfort zone.

Get Healthy

1. Be friendly with people from lots of different groups. It will prevent you from stereotyping

others and will build up your social skills so you'll be able to talk to just about anybody.

2. Invite people you normally don't hang out with to join your lunch table. It will expose your friends to new people even if they're not willing to make the effort. It will also send the message to others that you're open to making friends outside of your group.

3. Rework the way you think and talk about people. Instead of relying on stereotypes such as the "Korean girl" or the "skater chick," use more personal descriptions such as "Danielle who's good at math" or "Robin from the school play." Hopefully those around you will start seeing these people as individuals, too, rather than stereotyped members of various groups.

The Last Word from Thea

The media uses stereotypes as shortcuts and causes you to assume certain things about a character based on her clothes, friends, or skin color. As soon as the credits roll she's gone, but what's left is our habit of judging people we don't know based on what we see at first glance. Having a diverse group of friends is a great thing to do for yourself. When you're well-rounded, those around you will be inspired to try new things as well.

6

Getting Noticed

It's everywhere you turn. From the commercial selling herbal shampoo to the one selling exercise equipment, sex is all over the media. It is splashed across television and movie screens, magazine covers, billboards, and Web sites. The point is clear: sex sells. But is it something you really want to be buying?

Despite the constant blast of media messages, along with the stories flying through the school hallways, not all young people are having sex. In fact, according to national surveys, the number of kids in seventh to ninth grade who are sexually active is dropping each year. You may hear gossip about who is having sex, but don't believe everything you hear. It is certainly not true that everyone's doing it.

Tanya's friends aren't having sex yet, but they are going a lot further with their boyfriends than she wants to go. Is she just being very uncool and old-fashioned for wanting to wait?

Tanya's Story

Tanya glanced over at Logan as he opened his locker. The best thing about this school year was that her locker was only six away from his. She'd had a crush on Logan since the day she had met him in fourth grade.

"Hey, Logan, what's up?" she tried to ask casually as he pulled textbooks out of his backpack.

"Oh, hey, Tanya," he replied. He grinned one of those killer grins that made her stomach do flip-flops. "How ya doin'?"

Before Tanya could answer, Logan's eyes had

You may hear gossip about who is having sex, but don't believe everything you hear. It is certainly not true that everyone's doing it.

already looked beyond her, and she knew that either Carmen or Candy had to be standing behind her. Logan's face was pink, and his eyes were wide. Those two girls, with their short skirts and low-cut tops, always managed to do that to him.

"Logan! You're looking good this morning," said Carmen in that sleazy way of hers. Tanya knew that to Logan, she had just turned invisible.

Talk About It

- Why is Tanya's stomach doing flip-flops? Do you know that feeling?

- Have you ever had a crush on someone for a long time? Did that person notice you? What happened?

- Have you had a moment when you felt invisible to others? What made you feel that way?

All afternoon Tanya kept thinking about how differently Logan had responded to her than to Carmen and Candy. What did he see in them? Both of them had such nasty reputations. Wait a minute . . . was that *why* Logan liked them? Did he want a girl who looked and acted like they did?

That weekend, although Tanya would have preferred to be outside riding her bike, she spent hours and hours watching all the television shows that were being talked about at school. It was very clear on each episode that the girls who got the boys' attention were not the quiet ones such as Tanya. They didn't work hard on their grades. They didn't worry about doing their chores. They didn't wear their older sister's hand-me-downs and what they found at the local thrift store. They were nothing like her. Instead, they wore sexy clothes and always knew the right thing to say to make the boys want them.

Maybe I've been going about this all wrong, thought Tanya. Maybe I've had the wrong priorities. Maybe, just maybe, it's time for a change.

On Monday morning, Tanya's alarm clock went off 30 minutes earlier than usual. She wanted the extra time to pick out an outfit and to spend more time on her makeup and hair. It was time for a new look!

Talk About It

- Why does Tanya think that Carmen and Candy's reputations might be the reason Logan likes them?

- Why does she spend so much time watching popular television shows? What lessons are they teaching her?

- What television shows do you watch? What do they teach you about how girls your age should talk and behave? Do you tend to imitate what you see?

More than an hour later, Tanya took a final look at herself in the mirror. She was hot! The tiny top she had borrowed from her sister's closet showed off her belly button. The skirt that she hadn't worn before because it seemed too short now seemed just right. She had added her only pair of heels so she'd look more like the characters on the television shows. Best of all, Tanya had done an amazing job with her makeup. She looked at least 16 or 17 years old

When Tanya walked into school that morning, she could see some of the students watching her.

now, and even though it felt weird to have so much makeup on her face, it was worth it.

When Tanya walked into school that morning, she could see some of the students watching her. She grinned. She couldn't wait to see the look on Logan's face. She hurried over to her locker just as he was opening his.

"Morning, Logan," she said as casually as she could. "How are ya?"

"Hey, Tanya, I'm chill," he replied. He glanced over at her and then did a double take. "What happened to you?" he asked. "You look really . . ."

He paused. Tanya held her breath. What would he say?

" . . . different," he continued, frowning.

Tanya was confused. At first she had thought he liked her new look, but now she wasn't sure.

"It's just that, you know," he continued. "I didn't think you were one of those girls. Do you really want some of the guys talking about you the way they do about Carmen?"

Suddenly, Tanya felt ridiculous. "What do you mean?" she asked.

"If you're gonna dress like that, people are gonna think you follow through," replied Logan.

Maybe, Tanya thought, Logan didn't like that type of girl after all.

Talk About It

- What did Logan mean when he told Tanya that people would expect her to "follow through"?

- Is Logan someone Tanya should want to date?

- Have you ever decided to change your look? What do the clothes you wear tell people about who you are?

The day you start liking boys is the day that nothing else seems to matter nearly as much. It's perfectly fine to want to attract your crush, and part of how you do that is to look your best. But remember—it's *your* best—not what you think he'd like you to look like. If he doesn't like you for who you are already, then he's not the right guy for you. If you want to fix your hair, put on a little makeup, and wear your favorite outfit, that's fine. But trying to make yourself look older and sexier is not okay—your new look could send the wrong signals, and what the boy might end up liking is not you but what he thinks you're willing to put out. Stay true to who you are; that way, the people you attract will be the ones who appreciate you and not a phony, media-hyped version of who you think you have to be.

Get Healthy

1. Just because the sleazy girls get the guys on television doesn't mean it works that way all the time in real life. You can attract guys without showing skin or trying to look older and hotter. Some boys may go for that type of girl, but other boys will know to look further than that.

2. Don't believe the stories and rumors that everyone is having sex. In fact, most kids your age are not having sex. They are making it up and telling lies in an attempt to look older and more mature—and it does neither.

3. Having a crush on a boy is very normal. Flirting to get his attention is normal, too! Just remember that if you try too hard, you may not only send the wrong message to boys, but you may be creating an image of yourself that isn't really who you are.

The Last Word from Thea

Always remember that what you see in the media isn't the way it is in real life. The girls you see who always seem able to hook the boys are just actresses reading some lines they were given. In addition, the stories that you hear whispered in the restroom or passed by IM from student to student are often not true either.

Make smart decisions about what you do with your body and take responsibility for the choices you make regarding sex. Decide what you are comfortable with, which may mean choosing abstinence. Remember to watch out for yourself and think through the decisions you make. Learning to do that will get you far!

7

Older Crowd

atch enough movies and shows and you will quickly come to the conclusion that drinking and doing drugs is just part of the growing-up experience. Although sometimes you see how these kinds of behavior can lead to trouble and heartache, often what happens on-screen suggests that alcohol and drugs are the ticket you need to get popular, get noticed, get a boy, get loose, and get happy. In reality, they are much more likely to help you get puking, get addicted, get raped, get a disease, or get pregnant.

Both drugs and alcohol affect your personality. They can cloud your judgment and make you much more willing to do things that you normally wouldn't. While branching out and trying new things is usually a great thing to do, it isn't a smart idea if those behaviors are dangerous. Mental processes are slowed, inhibitions go away, and your guard comes down when you use drugs or alcohol. Think about the possible consequences of those side effects, and those substances quickly lose any appeal!

> **While branching out and trying new things is usually a great thing to do, it isn't a smart idea if those behaviors are dangerous.**

Julia found this out the hard way. Her older sister Camille invited her to go to a party with her, and Julia couldn't wait. She was sure she would remember this as the best night of her life—and she was half right. She will always remember it.

Julia's Story

Julia simply could not believe Cam was letting her go to the party with her. After all, she was only in eighth grade, and Cam was already in high school and driving. Of course, she knew it was because Cam had promised to stay with her that weekend while their parents went out of town, and the only way she could do that and still go to the party was to drag Julia along. But still . . . Julia was thrilled. She had been thinking about what to wear for the entire week. She was hoping people would think she was the same age as Cam instead of three years younger.

"What about this?" she asked Cam, turning around to show off an outfit she was thinking about wearing to the party.

Cam barely glanced up from her computer screen. "Whatever," she said. "Just don't embarrass me."

Talk About It

- **Why is Julia so excited about the party?**

- **Have you ever had the chance to go to a party or a dance where everyone was older than you were? What happened?**

- **Why is it so important to Julia to look older for the party? What would you do?**

The night of the party finally arrived. Cam and Julia's parents had left an hour earlier and wouldn't be back until the next night.

When the girls got to the party, Julia was shocked at how loud it was and how many people could fit into one house. She didn't recognize anyone there, and Cam had ditched her the minute they walked in. She stood in a corner and just watched everyone. In the kitchen, there was a huge silver keg of beer and bottles of alcohol on the counters.

"Hey, what's up? I'm Jason," a boy said to Julia. She tried to come up with a quick, casual answer, but

it felt as if her tongue was tied in knots, and all she managed was a nod. The boy shrugged his shoulders and walked away. Julia felt horrible. What was her problem? Why couldn't she just relax? Just then she thought of the movie she had recently watched. The uptight girl in that flick had downed a couple of beers, and suddenly she was the life of the party. Maybe that would work for her. She headed for the kitchen.

The beer tasted awful. Julia had to force down the first three swallows. How could people actually like this stuff? she wondered. Swallow by swallow, however, she got it down, and by the time she was finished, she was feeling a lot more comfortable. In fact, when Jason walked by this time, she smiled at him and said, "Hey, let's try that again." He grinned back as the two of them found a seat on the couch.

The beer tasted awful. Julia had to force down the first three swallows.

Julia talked and talked with Jason. She was amazed at how easy it was, and Jason seemed to think everything she said was interesting and funny.

"Hey, let me get you a drink," he said. "I'll bring you something that tastes a lot better than beer."

When Jason came back a few minutes later, he handed her a glass that looked like a soda with ice. When she took a sip, Julia could tell there was some

kind of alcohol in it, but it tasted so much better than the beer, she didn't care. She gulped most of it down. She was surprised a few minutes later to find she was not talking to Jason anymore; she was kissing him. She threw her legs over his and moved closer. No wonder Cam said making out was fun—this was great!

Julia kept kissing Jason, and although she could feel his hands slipping down her shirt and into the back of her jeans, she didn't stop him. She felt like she was floating in a fog, and everything seemed a little unreal. She didn't protest when Jason led her upstairs.

The next thing Julia knew she was on her back on a bed and Jason was tearing her shirt open and then tugging at the zipper on her jeans. Something flickered in the back of her head that she might be in trouble, but it felt like too much effort to say anything.

Just then, the door to the bedroom burst open, and Cam was standing there. Julia knew she was yelling about something called "roofies," but it was much easier to just close her eyes and drift away. What a night to remember.

Talk About It

- Why doesn't Julia stop Jason from doing things she knows she shouldn't allow him to do?

- Have you ever had a moment where you felt like you were no longer in control of a situation? What happened?

- What can you do to protect yourself from getting in a situation like Julia did?

Things that taste nasty usually are. When they are really being honest, most girls would tell you that they got sick from their first inhale on a cigarette or couldn't stand the taste of beer. So, why do they do it again? Because they think they have to in order to be cool or to seem more grown-up. If you are really being honest with yourself, you probably know that none of that is true.

In Julia's case, Jason slipped rohypnol, the date-rape drug, into her drink. Rohypnol pills, which are known as "roofies," were first used as a sleep aid but also cause forgetfulness. Rohypnol lowers inhibitions and causes muscles to relax, making girls who unknowingly take it easy targets for guys looking to take advantage of them. That's why roofies are also known as the date-rape drug.

Don't stay in a situation where you do not feel comfortable, including parties and sleepovers where kids are doing things that you know aren't good for you or aren't legal. Partying with an older crowd can seem glam, but you could be putting yourself in real danger. Julia was really lucky that her sister found her in time. Who's watching your back? Remember, your first priority is to be safe. Make sure you are with people who will help protect you from harmful situations.

Get Healthy

1. Wanting to fit in and run with the older kids is natural, but you may not be ready for the risks it might bring. Always have someone with you who will watch your back.

2. Never accept a drink at a party that you did not get yourself. If you drink a soda, make sure that you use an unopened can or bottle so nothing could have been added to it. If you leave your drink somewhere, don't go back and start drinking it—get a new one.

3. Being popular shouldn't ever be about becoming someone you aren't. If that's what it takes, it isn't worth it.

The Last Word from Thea

Depending on anything outside yourself to make people like you is a mistake, whether it's wearing only certain clothes, listening to specific music, or using drugs or alcohol. As Julia discovered, drinking might have made her relax—but it also made her do things she normally wouldn't have and exposed her to even bigger risks by lowering her ability to make decisions. Pass up the risk and bring along a buddy you trust to make sure you won't do anything you'll regret the next day.

8

Shoot 'Em Up

Face it. Violence is everywhere. If you don't hear it reported in graphic details on the nightly news, you can see it on some of the most popular television shows. Of course, if that isn't enough, you have another endless source of every kind of violence from guns and bombs to swords and axes: video games.

Games for all systems that are rated "Teen" and "Mature"—Wii, PlayStation, Xbox 360, and more—are bursting with every kind of violence possible. Players pull out monsters' body parts, soldiers shoot enemies in the head, characters get impaled on swords, and cutting off heads is typical. It is hard to believe that being exposed to violence—even unrealistic kinds—on a daily basis doesn't warp your attitude at least a little.

Megan had been hanging out with her brother and his friends for several months. She liked kidding around with them and playing video games with them. She had gotten quite good at the racing game and the shooting games. In fact, she was so good at them that she had begun to wonder how well she might shoot a real gun.

It is hard to believe that being exposed to violence—even unrealistic kinds—on a daily basis doesn't warp your attitude at least a little.

Megan's Story

Megan's finger flew over the game controller. She stared at the screen, giving a little cheer each time she massacred more enemies. Even though they were coming at her from all directions, she blasted every single one. "Go me!" shouted Megan as she blew away the last soldier. She jumped up and gave high fives to her brother and all of his friends and then did a little victory dance. "I did it, I did it," she sang. The guys weren't nearly as enthusiastic, though—frankly, they were getting tired of losing to her all the time. She really was good at these shooting games. Three months ago she had not even known how to work the controller. Now, she was beating all of them!

"Thanks for letting me play today, guys!" said Megan. "I gotta head out, though." She headed to her room to do her homework. I wish I were as good at geometry as I am at shooting, she thought. It sure would make school easier.

Talk About It

- **Why are the boys less than thrilled with Megan?**

- **Have you played video games before? How did you do? How did other players react to how well you played?**

- **Do you have a talent that is usually seen as something boys are supposed to be good at? How do girls react? How about boys?**

That weekend, Megan visited her grandparents' farm out in the country. She loved being there. It was so different from life in the city. It was still noisy, but instead of traffic and people, the sounds came from roosters and other farm animals.

On Sunday morning, while her grandparents were out feeding the chickens and collecting eggs, Megan crawled up into the attic to do some exploring. Her Grandpa Jim had told her to go ahead but to be careful. Every box she opened and went through had something interesting in it. She found a stack of old photo albums, bundles of letters that Grandpa Jim had written to Grandma Marge during the war, and even a box of old clothes that were almost cool enough to wear again today. Megan tried a few on and made a pile of the ones she liked the best. She hoped Grandma Marge would let her borrow them.

In the bottom of the last box she went through, Megan found something else. It was a BB gun. There were boxes of ammunition to go with it. She picked it up and held it in her hand. She began pretending she was playing the game she played at home, aiming at made-up enemies and monsters. "Bam, bam, bam!" she said, taking out three soldiers hiding in the back of the attic. She grinned. She could not wait to show this to the guys Monday after school. She snuck the gun downstairs and into her suitcase before Grandpa Jim could spot it.

Talk About It

- Why do you think Megan is so interested in the gun? Why does she hide it from her grandpa?

- Have you ever taken something without asking for permission first? What happened? How did you feel about it later?

On Monday afternoon, Megan plopped down on the beanbag chair between her brother Kyle and two of his friends. "Ready to play?" asked Kyle.

"Well, yeah, but not the usual game," replied Megan. She pulled the BB gun out from behind the couch, where she had hidden it. It was already loaded.

"Whoa! Look at that," said Peter in disbelief.

"Can I hold it?" asked Sean.

"Where in the world did you get that, Meg?" asked Kyle with a frown.

"I found it in Grandpa's attic," she explained. "I thought it would be fun to play with something real for a change. Let's take it out to the backyard."

Megan and the three boys went out the back door. "Let's see how good your aim really is," said Peter.

Megan pointed the BB gun at the tree nearest to them. "I bet I can shoot the bottom branch of that tree," she said. "Watch this."

She took careful aim. Just as she was about to pull the trigger, Copper, the family's black lab, came around the corner and startled her. She fired. The BB hit one of Copper's back legs. He fell to the ground, and Megan could see the blood gushing out of the wound. She dropped the gun and crouched down next to Copper, crying. "Get help, Kyle!" she shouted. "Get Mom now!"

She swore never to touch a gun—even a virtual one—ever again.

She glanced over at the BB gun on the patio. She swore never to touch a gun—even a virtual one—ever again.

Talk About It

- **What lesson did Megan learn?**

- **Have you ever tried something in real life that you have done in a game? Did it work? How was it different?**

- **Do you know anyone who has a gun? Have you ever held one? How did it feel?**

Movies, television shows, and even your favorite songs all make violence seem almost glamorous. Video and computer games give you the opportunity to be violent and improve your skill using all kinds of weapons. But being a good shot on a video game doesn't have anything to do with real life. In the real world, weapons do real damage, and the people who are attacked don't have the chance to get up and play that scene again. The better the graphics in video games get and the more realistic the special effects in the movies become, the more important it is for you to keep in mind the difference between fantasy and reality. Megan's big mistake was in trying to turn her virtual world into reality, with a dangerous outcome.

In the real world, the people who carry guns, such as police officers and military personnel, hope they never have to use them. The people trained in martial arts will tell you that they would only use their lethal weapons as a last resort for protection. And in the real world, the people who choose to be violent, use their weapons, and attack others end up behind bars.

You have the power to decide what you watch, what you play, and what you do. You don't have to expose yourself to violence. You can change the channel, pick the kind of movie you want to see, and choose the music that you listen to. What kind of world do you want to live in? You get to choose.

Get Healthy

1. Although violence is a part of modern life, that doesn't mean it has to have a major role in your life. Choose games that focus on speed and skill rather than violence.

2. If you watch violent movies or television shows, keep in mind that it is fiction. In real life, those people getting killed would have been someone's child, parent, or sibling.

3. Never handle any kind of weapon. They are more dangerous than you would ever expect. If you are curious about them, ask your parents or get permission to do some online research. Do not, under any circumstances, handle them yourself.

The Last Word from Thea

We live in a violent world. We see violence all over the news. As much fun as games can be, it is critical to remember that violence hurts people. It isn't funny; it's painful. While you and other players can blow each other up multiple times or get shot with countless bullets, real life isn't like that, and knowing the difference is part of becoming an adult.

9

Born to Be Bad

Is there anything juicier than yet another story on the news about what a certain celeb has done now? Another ticket for drunken driving or disorderly conduct? How about public nudity? Did he punch out the paparazzi? Instead of being shocked and disgusted, many young people are impressed. What a cool thing to do—even if it means time in jail. Man, it's great to be bad, isn't it? Behaving badly has become a badge of honor in many girls' eyes—it's a ticket to instant fame.

While most of the things these celebrities do may look glamorous and exciting on television, if you tried them in real life, you'd probably be in big trouble with your parents and possibly your teachers. You'd also be stuck with the consequences of what you've done, and usually those are no fun at all. Being grounded by your parents or expelled from school are only the start of the consequences of bad behavior. Dealing with a bad reputation can make it harder to make friends or get a part-time job.

Brit was about to flirt with bad behavior. She and her friends took turns hosting sleepovers each month.

Being grounded by your parents or expelled from school are only the start of the consequences of bad behavior.

During her turn, a fun game of Truth or Dare leads her to make a decision that she may have to live with for quite a while.

Brit's Story

"Anyone want the last piece of pepperoni pizza?" asked Brit, holding the cardboard box.

"No way, I'm stuffed," said Leslie.

"Me, too," agreed Crista.

"You guys wanna watch a movie now or play Truth or Dare?" asked Brit. She already knew which they would pick.

"Truth or Dare, of course," said Celine. Everyone agreed.

The girls sat in a circle. In Brit's opinion, this was always the best part of the sleepovers. The truth questions were great because they learned secrets and stories about each other. The dares, however, were her favorite because it was so funny to see her friends do stupid things, such as wearing a bra they had put in the freezer or running into the other room to give Brit's surprised brother a kiss on the cheek.

Talk About It

- **Why does Brit enjoy Truth or Dare so much?**
- **Have you ever played the game? Did you enjoy it?**
- **If you play, do you usually choose truth or dare? Why?**

"OK, um . . . Leslie," said Crista. "Truth or dare?"

Leslie hesitated and then said, "Truth."

"I got an IM last week saying that you had cheated on your math test. Is that true?"

"That is *so* not true!" said Leslie. "Damian, you know the football player . . . well, he leaned over and asked me a question during the test. Mr. Harmon turned around just as I said I couldn't talk to him. I was *not* cheating."

"What did Damian ask you?" asked Brit curiously.

"Ha! You'll have to wait and ask me on the next round," said Leslie with a giggle as she stuck her tongue out at the other girls. They all laughed.

"Now . . . Brit," said Leslie. "Truth or dare?"

Brit always chose truth because dares were kind of scary. She knew everyone was waiting for her to say it, so she surprised them all and said, "Dare!"

"Okay!" said Leslie. "Umm . . . lemme think. Oh, I know! I dare you to go in the bathroom, get your dad's electric razor, and shave a strip of your hair off. Either side or on top is okay. I mean, a lot of the stars are doing it, so you will be way cool!"

There was silence in the room. No dare had ever been this drastic before. Brit felt her face get hot. Now what was she supposed to do? She had chosen dare, but she hadn't planned on anything like this. All the other girls were staring at her.

Talk About It

- Why are Brit and the other girls so surprised at Leslie's dare?

- Has anyone ever dared you to do something that scared you or made you uncomfortable? What did you do?

- What kind of consequences might Brit face if she accepts this dare?

Brit stared at herself in the bathroom mirror. She could hear the murmur of the other girls talking in her bedroom. She knew they were just waiting to see what she would do.

She held her dad's electric razor in her hand. She looked at her hair. It was blonde and wavy and reached about halfway down her back. It was definitely her favorite feature and one of the few things she actually liked about herself. How could she possibly cut off a whole section of it? What would her parents say?

On the other hand, how could she not? The other girls would think she was a wuss for not following through. It would be embarrassing, and maybe they wouldn't want to have sleepovers with her anymore. And Leslie was right. A bunch of the popular actors and singers were doing radical things like this with their hair.

What should she do?

Finally, she turned on the razor. She held it in her hand and tried to decide where the best place to start would be. Should she do it on the left or the right? She thought about doing it in the middle but that was too extreme for her. She held up a lock of her hair on the left side and took a deep breath. Here I go, she thought.

Suddenly, there was a pounding on the door. "Brit! Brit!" screamed Leslie. "What are you doing? It was a joke, for heaven's sake! Don't do it! Not your beautiful hair!" She threw open the door.

Talk About It

- **Why does Brit hesitate to do the dare? What do you think about her reasons for almost doing it?**

- **How do you think she feels in the end? How do you feel about what happened?**

- **Have you ever made a decision with serious consequences? How did you decide? How did you feel at the time? Later?**

The media is so much hype. It can turn anything into a great story. Some celebs can get arrested, and all their fans might run to their rescue. Others can do something outrageous—like shave their heads—and it becomes the new fashion statement. In the real world, there are real consequences, and no one is going to think you are fab for shaving your head, getting arrested, or getting pregnant. Trying to fashion yourself after your favorite celeb may turn your life into a disaster.

Taking dares also can be disastrous. Lots of kids who thought they were being brave took dares that ended their lives. And, there are kids who took dares for fun and end up really screwing up their lives. If Brit had really taken the dare, she would have been miserable. She probably would have been too embarrassed to show her face, her friends may not have wanted to be seen with her, and her parents no doubt would have been furious with her for caving to a foolish dare.

Before you take a dare, think about the worst thing that could happen. If it doesn't seem too bad, and actually seems like fun, then go for it. But if you can imagine the possibility of a really bad outcome, then choose to be the chicken with all your hair rather than a brave but bald eagle.

Get Healthy

1. Just because a celebrity does something awesome, it doesn't mean you should do it too. It's easy to think that because someone is famous, everything he or she does is cool, but sometimes it is just plain stupid.

2. When you are dared to do something, give it some real thought. Sometimes a dare can make you break out of your shell and try something new, and that can be great. Other times, a dare can be something very dumb or dangerous. Impressing your friends isn't a good enough reason to cave.

3. Although your friends' opinions and ideas are important to you, make sure you are able to make up your own mind about things based on who you are and not on what they think.

The Last Word from Thea

The world is full of famous people who have done amazingly stupid things. They behave terribly even though the whole world is watching. Chances are, if you had the chance to talk one-on-one with any of them a few years down the road, they would be embarrassed at their actions. While the fans may think a celeb's behavior is cool and daring, the reality may be that it's just plain dumb.

10

Brand New

Somewhere along the way, advertisers started telling us that brand names are everything. Brand logos are designed to stick in our minds, so we'll recognize them anywhere. Ad executives try to make us feel that clothes with names or logos stitched on them will make us more important, more attractive, or more popular. But what makes a brand-name shirt different from a similar shirt without the brand? Not much, except the cost—buy by brand, and you will end up paying a high price. When people are willing to pay big bucks for name brands, companies win and customers lose.

Kaitlin was having a hard time with this very issue. She wanted to wear the same brands of clothes that her friends had, but her parents refused to go to those stores because they simply couldn't afford it and wouldn't want to spend that kind of money on a shirt or a pair of shoes even if they could. It was frustrating for Kaitlin, and she didn't know what to do.

Kaitlin's Story

"What are you wearing to the dance this weekend?" asked Jamie, as she posed in front of the mirror in Kaitlin's bedroom. She turned each way, modeling her brand new jeans. Kaitlin had to admit they looked fantastic on Jamie. It just made Kaitlin envy her even more.

"I'm not sure yet," she finally replied. The truth was she was hoping that before the dance that weekend she would be able to get a new pair of jeans from a trendy store at the mall. She had asked her mother for the last two weeks, and although she kept getting a firm no, Kaitlin was holding out that her mom would change her mind.

Kaitlin wished most of her jeans and shirts could come from some of the mall stores where her friends shopped.

Although Kaitlin didn't mind getting her socks, underwear, and even her shoes at discount stores, she wished most of her jeans and shirts could come from some of the mall stores where her friends shopped. It just didn't seem fair.

Talk About It

- Why is Kaitlin jealous of her friend Jamie? Have you ever been jealous of something your friend had that you didn't have?

- Why does Kaitlin feel that her parents are treating her unfairly?

- Have you ever wanted something that your parents wouldn't agree to buy? How did you feel about it? What did you do?

"Mom, can we go to the mall this afternoon?" Kaitlin asked the following day.

"Why? What do you need?" asked Mrs. Simmons absentmindedly.

Kaitlin sighed. Here we go again, she thought. "I wanted to check out those jeans I told you about before," she said. "Remember? I wanted to wear them for the dance this weekend."

This time it was her mom's turn to sigh. "Kaitlin," she said, "I've told you repeatedly that I am not going to pay as much for a pair of jeans as I do for a week's worth of groceries. That is just ridiculous. We don't have that much money to spare for things like that. If you want a new pair of jeans, I might be able to manage that—but not from that store."

Kaitlin slammed her hand on the kitchen table. "That is just not fair, Mom!" she yelled. "Don't you know how important this is to me? I have to look great for the dance. You just don't care, do you?" She stormed out of the kitchen and into her bedroom, slamming the door behind her.

Talk About It

- **What do you think of Kaitlin's reaction to her mom?**
- **Are there other solutions to Kaitlin's problem? Was there another way she could have handled it?**

That Friday, Kaitlin watched as the clock flipped to 6:00 p.m. The school dance was going to begin in an hour. If she was going to go, it was time to get dressed. *I guess I could wear the jeans I got last week,* she thought. *I haven't worn them to school yet, so at least they would be new.*

She opened her closet door. She pulled out the shirt she had been saving for weeks to wear to the dance. She then reached back in and began searching for her jeans. Suddenly she spotted something she didn't recognize. She pulled out the hanger and gasped. It was a pair of the jeans she wanted! Where had they come from? How did they get in her closet? She tried them on, and they fit just as perfectly as she had pictured.

It was a pair of the jeans she wanted! Where had they come from?

"Hey, they look great," said Mrs. Simmons, standing in the doorway.

"Where did they come from?" asked Kaitlin. "Did you get them for me?"

"Sure did," said her mom.

"But . . . why did you change your mind? Did you win the lottery or something?"

"Huh! I wish," laughed Mrs. Simmons. "Actually, I was turning in some old clothes of your brothers at the thrift store today, and I checked if they had the brand of jeans you like so much. I was amazed to find them—and even more amazed to get them for only $8.99."

Kaitlin frowned. The jeans were great—but they weren't new. Would anyone know? She took another look in the mirror. No way. They looked fantastic. "This is going to be our secret," she said to her mom. Then she gave her a huge hug. "Thanks, Mom. This was the best surprise ever."

Talk About It

- Why does Kaitlin want to keep where the jeans came from a secret? Does it change how she feels about the jeans?

- What do you think about the price of most brand-name clothes? Do you prefer to wear them and not others? If so, why?

Brand names are popular because most girls—and let's face it, even most women—want to be fashionable and up to date with the styles. That's great for the look, but not necessarily for the wallet. The reality is that brand names are usually very expensive—especially in their own stores and in the upscale malls. But, sometimes they can be found in other places such as thrift shops or consignment stores or stores that carry brand names at discount prices. There's nothing like a bargain to feel that shopping satisfaction.

Scout out the sales, and learn how to be a good shopper. If your funds are limited, think about the articles of clothing that are most important to you. If you really want to have a certain brand, it might be best to go for the items that you can wear or use a lot, such as shoes, a purse, or a jacket. Or, maybe it's the earrings or the wallet that carry the logo and fit your budget. Finding a way to be stylish and not spend a whole wad of cash can be a fun challenge. Plus, you can enjoy the fact that the mall girls spent a ton and you did it on the cheap.

Get Healthy

1. Check out thrift stores and consignment shops, as they often have brand-name clothing for far cheaper. You can actually

make it a contest to see what hidden treasures might be hanging on a rack.

2. If you want brand-name clothes that your parents think are too expensive, you may have to be willing to help pay for them. Save your allowance, save birthday and holiday money, be willing to babysit, or help with chores to earn extra cash.

3. Perhaps your parents would be agreeable to giving you a set amount of money for your clothes. Then, it could be up to you to spend it any way you want. Just remember the more you spend on one item of clothing, the less you'll have to spend on others.

The Last Word from Thea

Wanting to wear the hottest fashions is completely understandable. Balancing your desires with the amount of money you have to spend is just plain old reality. Some families have more money than others, but that doesn't mean you can't be stylish. You may simply need to be more creative in where you shop, what you buy, and how you can earn money. There are lots of ways to help stretch your dollar. Learning to be a good shopper and bargain hunter are great skills to develop now and to have as you become a grown woman and go out on your own, having to buy all of your own clothes.

A Second Look

There is nothing wrong with wanting to look your best. Wearing makeup, buying new clothes, and experimenting with your hair are really exciting parts of being a girl. Reading magazines, going to movies, and watching your favorite television shows with your friends are all a part of being a teenager. The problems arise, however, when you start to compare yourself to everyone around you, or even worse—to the unrealistic images you see all over the media.

Like we've seen in the stories in this book, a girl who tries to act out what she sees on television or in the movies is in for some real trouble. The plotlines in these forms of entertainment have to be over the top, otherwise they wouldn't be interesting to watch! On another note, looking at perfect actors and actresses can make you feel really down about yourself if you don't step back and look at the big picture. These people are not perfect, and neither are you—and that's okay!

Learning to separate fact from fiction is a real mark of maturity. Thinking for yourself is a great skill to learn! The media, however, wants you to think a certain way, and that is usually destructive. Commercials and advertisements want you to feel inadequate and unattractive so that you'll buy their products. Otherwise, they wouldn't make much money, would they?

So while you can have fun buying clothes and makeup, remember that your outside appearance is not the most important thing. Spend time developing yourself from the inside out by reading, writing, studying, and making friends with many types of people.

Looks fade fast, so spend time working on your inner character. This will never go out of style!

XOXO,
Thea

Pay It Forward

Remember, a healthful life is about balance. Now that you know how to walk that path, pay it forward to a friend or even to yourself! Remember the Get Healthy tips throughout this book, and then take these steps to get healthy and get going.

- Make a list of your favorite celebrities and why you like them. Do you look up to your favorite actress because she has admirable internal qualities, such as being smart or generous, or are you looking only at the outside? The media focuses mostly on external features, but there is much more to beauty than looks.

- If you want more privileges from your parents, prove to them that you have earned their trust. The way to earn their respect is by displaying your maturity through calm conversation, not through constant whining or yelling. If you show your parents you are more mature, they will be more likely to treat you that way.

- Trust your instincts. If something tastes bad or if a situation doesn't feel right, don't continue the behavior just to fit in. If you're uncomfortable with someone or something, don't feel like you have to stay in the situation.

- Make friends with many different types of people. Doing so will not only expand your social network, but also will expose you to many opportunities. It's a good idea to practice conversing with people from lots of different groups.

- Play video or computer games that focus on skill or teamwork instead of violence. Remember that video games do not accurately portray reality. Just like your favorite television shows and movies, they are not true to life and should not tell you how to act!

- Learn to eat right and exercise regularly. Treat your body well, because it will be with you for the rest of your life! Get together with a friend to ride bikes, take a walk, or rollerblade. These are great ways to be social and active at the same time.

- If you really must have a brand-name item of clothing, start a budget and save your money. This is an important skill to develop and will prepare you for financial independence when you are an adult.

Additional Resources

Select Bibliography

Kearney, Mary Celeste. *Girls Make Media*. New York: Routledge, 2006.

Lamb, Sharon, and Lyn Mikel Brown. *Packaging Girlhood: Rescuing Our Daughters from Marketers' Schemes*. New York: St. Martin's Press, 2007.

Quart, Alissa. *Branded: The Buying and Selling of Teenagers*. New York: Basic Books, 2004.

Richardson, Brenda Lane, and Elane Rehr. *101 Ways to Help Your Daughter Love Her Body*. New York: HarperCollins, 2001.

Further Reading

Bradley, Linda, and M. LaVora Perry. *Teen Sisters' Health: A Wellness Guide for Body, Mind, and Spirit*. Cleveland, OH: Cleveland Clinic Press, 2008.

Brashich, Audrey D. *All Made Up: A Girl's Guide to Seeing Through Celebrity Hype to Celebrate Real Beauty*. New York: Walker Books, 2006.

Lewis, Barbara A. *What Do You Stand For? For Teens: A Guide To Building Character*. Minneapolis, MN: Free Spirit Publishing, 2005.

Web Sites

To learn more about media messages and social norms, visit ABDO Publishing Company on the World Wide Web at **www.abdopublishing.com**. Web sites about media messages and social norms are featured on our Book Links page. These links are routinely monitored and updated to provide the most current information available.

For More Information

For more information on this subject, contact or visit the following organizations.

Hardy Girls Healthy Women

PO Box 821, Waterville, ME 04903-0821
207-861-8131
www.hghw.org
Focusing not only on young women, but also on the society that influences today's adolescents, this national program teaches safety, independence, and equality. It also promotes the importance of these values within the social contexts of girls' lives.

New Moon

2 West First Street, #101, Duluth, MN 55802
800-381-4743 or 218-728-5507
www.newmoongirlmedia.com
Creators of an advertisement-free publication for girls, this group seeks to encourage girls to speak up and be heard.

Glossary

abstinence
A choice not to engage in sexual activity.

Afro
An African-American hairstyle of tight curls in a full, rounded shape.

biracial
Of, related to, or involving parents of two different races.

dehydrate
To have a lack of water in the body.

eating disorder
Irregular and unhealthy eating habits, often characterized by eating too little or too much.

illusion
Something that gives a false sense of reality.

instinct
A natural impulse or feeling.

media
Any of the methods of mass communication, including television, radio, newspapers, books, and magazines.

obsess
> To continually be preoccupied with or not stop focusing on a certain idea or thought.

paparazzi
> Photographers who take pictures of celebrities or other famous people.

retouch
> To alter or change a photograph, usually to improve it.

rohypnol
> Also known as the date-rape drug, rohypnol is a substance that causes muscle relaxation and forgetfulness.

stereotype
> A sweeping generalization about a person or a group of people, usually based on first impressions.

thrift store
> A store that sells secondhand goods at lower prices.

Index

About the Authors

Thea Palad has an extensive background in media, magazine, and journalistic writing. Her work has appeared in a number of women's publications. Coauthoring with Thea, Tamra Orr has written more than 100 educational books for young people and lives in the Pacific Northwest with her husband and four kids.

Photo Credits

Steph Fowler/Jupiterimages/AP Images, 12; Rob Melnychuk/Jupiterimages/AP Images, 15; Quavondo Nguyen/iStock Photo, 21; David Young-Wolff/Getty Images, 25; Nacivet/Getty Images, 30; Lisa Pines/Getty Images, 33; Joselito Briones/iStock Photo, 35; iStock Photo, 40, 88; Ken Reid/Getty Images, 43; Zia Soleil/ Getty Images, 51; Dennie Cody/Getty Images, 57; Image Source/Getty Images, 59; Donn Thompson/Getty Images, 61; Bob Stevens/Getty Images, 67; Adrian Weinbrecht/ Getty Images, 69; Glowimages/Getty Images, 71; Jenny Acheson/Getty Images, 76; Sean Ives/Getty Images, 78; Tina Lorien/iStock Photo, 81; SW Productions/Getty Images, 87; Dylan Ellis/Getty Images, 91; Simon Smith/ iStock Photo, 96; Ryan McVay/Getty Images, 99